NEVER
Smile at a
Monkey*

*And 17 other important things to remember

Steve Jenkins

Houghton Mifflin Harcourt • Boston • New York

Everyone knows that tigers, crocodiles, sharks, and other large predators are **dangerous.** Many smaller animals are also well-known threats. People do their best to avoid rattlesnakes, black widow spiders, and piranhas, to name just a few.

This book is about **creatures** — both large and small — whose dangerous nature may not be so obvious. Their **teeth, claws, spines,** and **venom** can be deadly to an unsuspecting or careless human.

What makes these animals so dangerous? And what should you **never** do if you encounter one of them?

NEVER
pet a platypus.

This peculiar-looking
animal appears
harmless, even
comical, as it waddles
about. The platypus,
however, is the only
poisonous mammal.
It has venomous spurs
on its hind legs, and
it can give you a very
painful jab.

If you notice one of these beautifully patterned shells on the sea floor, you might be tempted to pick it up. That would be a big mistake. The cone shell hunts and defends itself with poisoned barbs that can be launched like harpoons. The barbs are so poisonous that you can die within minutes of being stabbed.

NEVER collect a cone shell.

NEVER harass a hippopotamus.

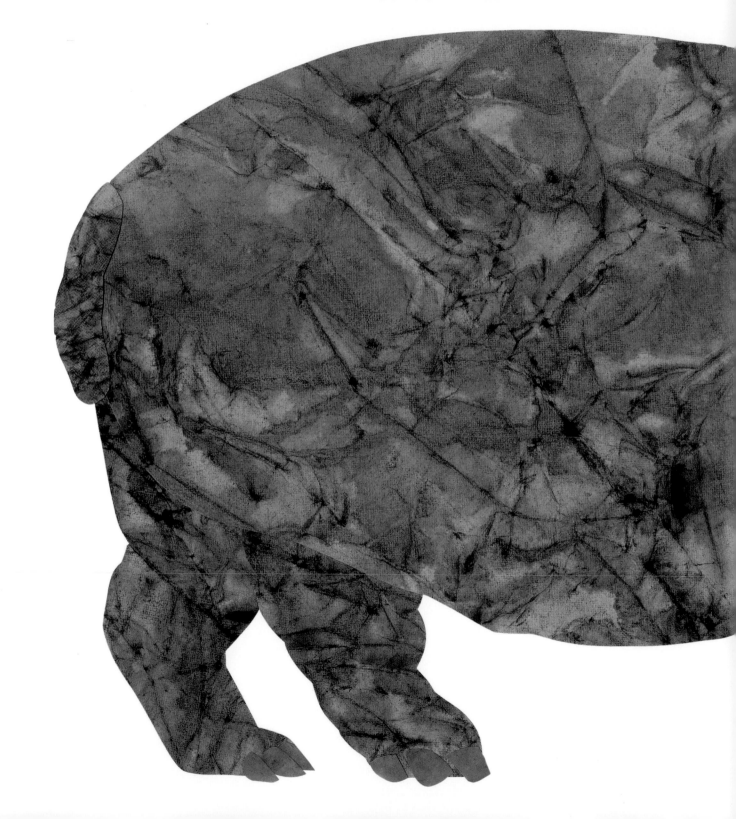

Hippos kill more people in Africa than any other wild animal. If a hippopotamus finds its path to the water blocked — or if it thinks that its baby is threatened — it will charge, attacking with an enormous mouth and long tusks.

A box jellyfish, that is. Most jellyfish can sting people, but the box jellyfish, also known as a sea wasp, is in a class by itself. Even the smallest contact with its stinging tentacles causes intense pain. If you are unlucky enough to become really entangled with a box jellyfish, you can die very quickly.

NEVER jostle a jellyfish.

NEVER
step on a
stingray.

Normally, stingrays do not attack people. But if you step on a ray or frighten it by swimming too close you can be seriously injured, or — if you're really unlucky — killed. The ray can drive its long, poisonous spine deep into the body of any animal or human that it perceives as a threat.

NEVER clutch a cane toad.

This large, homely amphibian is a gentle insect eater. It's harmless, except for two large sacs of venom on its neck. If pressed, these pouches squirt out a blinding, and sometimes deadly, poison.

NEVER

poach a puffer fish.

The puffer fish can inflate itself like a prickly balloon, but that's not what makes it so dangerous. This fish's flesh contains a deadly toxin, and unless you know exactly what you are doing, cooking and eating it can kill you.

NEVER
cuddle a cub.

Black bears try to avoid people and are rarely aggressive. One exception is a mother bear that thinks her cubs are in danger. Bear cubs are fuzzy and cute, and you might want to get a closer look or even — foolishly — try to pet one. Since the mother bear is usually nearby, this is not a good idea.

NEVER stare at a spitting cobra.

If you come across this hooded, hissing reptile, you'll probably suspect that it is dangerous. What you might not realize is that it can spit its venom accurately for more than eight feet (2½ meters). It aims for the eyes, and its poison can cause intense pain — even permanent blindness.

This colorful caterpillar will turn into a harmless brown moth. But until that happens, look out! If your skin touches its hairy bristles, you'll feel an intense burning sensation. Without immediate medical attention, weakness, severe illness, and death can follow.

NEVER
caress
an
electric
caterpillar.

NEVER corner a cassowary.

The cassowary is a flightless bird that stands as tall as a man. Though it is shy and avoids people, a surprised or cornered cassowary can deliver a lethal kick with its sharp claws.

NEVER
antagonize
an
African
buffalo.

The African buffalo, a relative of the domestic cow, is one of the most dangerous large animals in the world. It has sharp hooves, long horns, and an extremely nasty temper. It's not enough to just stay out of the African buffalo's way. If you are anywhere in its vicinity, this unpredictable animal may attack without warning.

NEVER touch a tang.

This coral reef fish has a razor-sharp spine on either side of its tail. If frightened, it whips its tail back and forth, slashing with its spines. The tang is a popular aquarium fish, but it must be handled with great care. Even a small tang can give you a serious injury, and a large tang can inflict life-threatening wounds.

This octopus is small enough to rest in the palm of your hand. Unfortunately, it is also one of the world's most poisonous animals. It can inflict a bite with a beak so sharp that at first you might not notice that you've been bitten. Without medical help, you can be killed by the venom of the blue-ringed octopus in less than an hour.

NEVER
bother a blue-ringed octopus.

NEVER confront a kangaroo.

The male kangaroo defends itself by boxing with its front legs or balancing on its tail and kicking out with its back feet. When it's really riled up, a kangaroo can deliver a kick powerful enough to cave in a person's chest.

This poisonous lizard
is normally slow
moving, but it can
react with surprising
speed if it is alarmed.
It latches on to prey,
predator, or unlucky
human with powerful
jaws. It doesn't have
fangs, so it chews its
venom into a bite
with its teeth.

NEVER
badger a beaded lizard.

NEVER
swim with a squid.

Especially not if it's a Humboldt squid. This fierce ocean predator can be longer than a full-grown man, and its tentacles are lined with thousands of sharp teeth. The Humboldt squid attacks at high speed, whipping its tentacles around a victim and tearing out chunks of flesh with a sharp, parrot-like beak.

And a final
word of advice:
NEVER
smile
at a monkey!

If you smile at a rhesus
(*ree-sus*) monkey, it
may interpret your
show of teeth as an
aggressive gesture and
respond violently.
Even a small monkey
can give you a serious
bite with its long,
sharp fangs.

To survive in the wild, animals must find or catch food. At the same time, they must avoid being killed by predators. To help them do this, the creatures in this book use weapons that have been developed over millions of years. The animals with the sharpest spines, fiercest bite, or most powerful venom are usually the ones most likely to survive and pass on these deadly qualities to their offspring. What makes these creatures so good at survival, however, can make them dangerous to an unwary human.

The **platypus** is about the size of a small housecat. It lives in eastern Australia, and it is one of two kinds of mammals that lay eggs rather than give birth to live babies (the other is the echidna). The platypus feeds on small aquatic animals and insects, using special electric receptors on its bill to detect the faint electric fields produced by its prey. The male platypus's poisonous spur isn't fatal to humans, but someone jabbed by a platypus can experience intense pain for weeks.

There are hundreds of different kinds of **cone shell**. All are poisonous. The deadliest is the geographic cone shell, which lives near coral reefs in the southwestern Pacific and Indian oceans. It is about six inches (15 centimeters) long, and gets its name from the map-like patterns on its shell. Cone shells are a kind of snail, and they move very slowly. When a cone shell spears a worm, fish, or other animal with its long, poisonous barb, its powerful venom kills the prey almost instantly, so it doesn't have time to struggle or swim away.

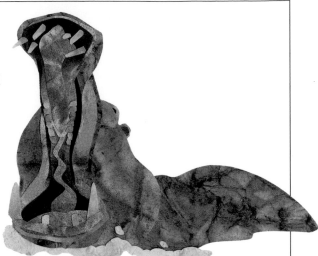

The **hippopotamus** spends much of its time in the water. Hippos live in central and southern Africa, where they gather in herds — also called bloats — of five to fifty animals. Hippos have sensitive skin. To stay cool and avoid being sunburned, they pass the daylight hours submerged in a lake or river, with just the top of their head sticking out of the water. At night they emerge to graze on grass and other plants. A large male hippo can weigh more than 6,000 pounds (2,700 kilograms). On land, only the elephant is larger. Hippos are territorial, and they fiercely protect a stretch of river they consider their own. This makes them extremely dangerous to any human who gets too close.

The **box jellyfish**, also known as the sea wasp, has the deadliest venom of any animal. More than 5,000 human deaths have been caused by contact with this jellyfish's stinging tentacles. Most jellyfish simply drift about on ocean currents, but the box jellyfish can swim quickly and actively pursues shrimp and small fish. It is also the only jellyfish with eyes — it has 24 of them arranged around the sides of its bell. Its sting kills prey almost instantly, preventing a struggling victim from escaping or damaging the jellyfish's delicate tentacles. The most dangerous species of box jellyfish has a bell about the size of a basketball and tentacles up to ten feet (3 meters) long. Green sea turtles feed on box jellyfish — they are immune to jellyfish poison.

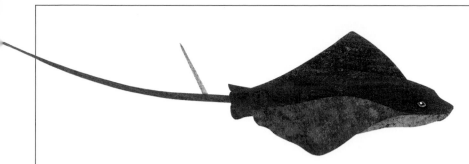

Cane toads are native to Central and South America but are best known in Australia. There, in 1935, farmers introduced them to eat beetles that attack sugar cane. They have since multiplied wildly, and are now considered a major pest. Many endangered Australian animals have been poisoned by trying to eat a cane toad. With their legs fully extended, cane toads can be 18 inches (46 centimeters) long. Like most toads, they feed on insects and small animals. They also eat human garbage, dog food, and dead animals.

Stingrays are found throughout the world in warm, shallow ocean water, often lying hidden in the sand. Rays, like their relatives the sharks, don't have bones. Their bodies are supported by cartilage — the same hard material you can feel inside your nose. Some stingrays are no larger than a person's hand. Others can be more than six and a half feet (2 meters) across and weigh almost 800 pounds (360 kilograms). Stingrays eat crabs, clams, and other small sea floor animals. The stingray protects itself with a sharp, venomous spine located at the base of its tail. On a large ray, this spine can be as long as a person's forearm.

There are more than 100 different species of **puffer fish**. The smallest could fit comfortably in a teaspoon; the largest is more than two feet (61 centimeters) long. They feed on algae and shellfish and are found in warm ocean waters around the world. To discourage predators, puffer fish suck in water and inflate themselves like a prickly balloon. If an attacker eats the puffer anyway, it will probably be killed by a strong poison in the puffer's body. The same toxin can be deadly to humans, who sometimes eat these fish. In Japan, puffer fish are called *fugu*. They are considered a delicacy, and only specially trained chefs are allowed to prepare them. Even then, a very small amount of poison remains in their flesh. People who eat *fugu* enjoy the tingling sensation this puffer fish poison creates on their lips and tongue.

Black bears can be found in 41 of the 50 United States, Canada, and northern Mexico. They are omnivores, feeding on roots, berries, seeds, fish, eggs, insects, and small animals — even deer or young elk. Female black bears weigh as much as 400 pounds (180 kilograms). Males are even larger, reaching 600 pounds (270 kilograms) or more. Black bear cubs, however, weigh less than a pound at birth — much less than a newborn human baby. Black bears have powerful claws and sharp teeth. They can swim, climb trees, and run almost as fast as a horse. It's a good thing that they are generally peaceful and avoid humans. There have been a few attacks on people by hungry bears, but bad encounters with these bears most often happen when a mother bear believes her cubs are threatened.

Several different species of **spitting cobra** live in Asia and Africa. The largest, recently discovered by scientists in Kenya, grows to nine feet (2¾ meters) in length. These poisonous snakes don't actually spit. They spray venom from forward-facing holes in their fangs, propelling it with a blast of air from their lungs. They can also use their fangs to inject venom, and a bite can prove fatal to a human. Spitting cobras eat frogs, birds, and small mammals.

The **electric caterpillar,** a type of stinging caterpillar, is the larva of a moth that lives in southern Brazil. This caterpillar doesn't sting like a bee or bite like a spider. Instead, its body is covered with fine, poison-filled spines. These spines break off and stick in the skin of anyone unlucky enough to touch them. Electric caterpillars can reach two inches (5 centimeters) in length. They eat the leaves of several different kinds of trees and shrubs.

The **cassowary** lives in New Guinea and northeastern Australia. It is the world's third tallest bird, after the ostrich and the emu. The cassowary has a bony "helmet" that gives it the distinction of being the only armored bird in the world. Females are larger than males, and can reach six and a half feet (2 meters) in height. The cassowary lives in dense forests and may use the bony crest on its head to push its way through the undergrowth. It defends itself by kicking and slashing with its feet. Cassowaries eat fruit, insects, frogs, and snakes.

African buffalo, also called Cape buffalo, gather in herds and graze on leaves and grass in the woodlands and open plains of central and southern Africa. A male can weigh 2,000 pounds (900 kilograms) — as much as a small car. African buffalo are short-tempered and unpredictable, and will charge any animal that appears to be a threat. They have been known to attack and kill a full-grown lion.

Tang, sometimes called surgeonfish, live near coral reefs throughout the world's oceans. These colorful fish feed on algae, and reach a maximum length of about 20 inches (50 centimeters). The tang defends itself with two sharp spines that grow near its tail. These spines normally lie flat against the tang's side, but can be extended and used as knifelike weapons if the fish feels threatened. Tang are popular aquarium fish, but they must be handled carefully to avoid cuts. A large, free-swimming tang can cut a diver deeply enough to cause fatal injuries.

The body of the **blue-ringed octopus** is the size of a Ping-Pong ball, and even with its eight tentacles outspread it is only about eight inches (20 centimeters) across. This tiny animal is one of the most poisonous creatures on earth. It makes its home in tide pools and reefs along the shores of the western Pacific Ocean from Australia to Japan, where it feeds on crabs and small fish with its sharp beak. The blue-ringed octopus is normally a yellow-brown color, but when it is frightened bright blue rings and spots appear on its skin.

There is no antidote for its poison, but if a victim can be kept alive with artificial respiration for 24 hours or so, they can recover from a bite without any ill effects.

All kangaroos are marsupials — females carry and nurse their young in a pouch. **Red kangaroos**, the largest of the kangaroos, are found throughout much of Australia. They average five feet (1½ meters) tall, but some males reach six and a half feet (2 meters) in height and can weigh 200 pounds (91 kilograms). Over short distances, a kangaroo can outrun a racehorse. It can also cover 25 feet (7½ meters) in a single leap. Kangaroos gather in groups, called mobs, to feed on grass and other plants. Male kangaroos are called jacks. Females are jills, and young kangaroos are joeys.

The **beaded lizard** is one of the world's few venomous lizards. The others are the Gila monster and the Komodo dragon. Beaded lizards live in the woodlands of Mexico and Guatemala. They eat bird and reptile eggs, along with the occasional small mammal, and may grow to three feet (91 centimeters) in length. For humans, a beaded lizard bite is extremely painful. On rare occasions, it can be lethal.

Humboldt squid are fast-swimming, aggressive predators. They live in the eastern Pacific Ocean, where they gather in schools of more than 1,000 animals. They feed on fish, shrimp, and other squid. Luckily, they usually stay in deep water, but human divers and fishermen in shallow water have been attacked. Though Humboldt squid are large, growing to lengths of six and a half feet (2 meters), they live for only about one year. They are also known as jumbo flying squid, because they sometimes jet from the water and glide through the air for several yards to escape danger.

Rhesus (*ree-sus*) monkeys live in the grasslands and forests of India and Southeast Asia. In the wild they eat fruit, leaves, and small animals, but they have also become a pest in many human cities, where they steal food, rummage through garbage, and sometimes threaten people. These primates live in groups, or troops, that may include hundreds of monkeys. They have a complex social structure, and use sounds, gestures, and facial expressions to communicate with each other. Rhesus monkeys are about 20 inches (51 centimeters) long and weigh around 15 pounds (7 kilograms).

For further reading:

101 Questions and Answers About Dangerous Animals.
By Seymour Simon. Simon & Schuster Children's Publishing, 1995.

Dangerous Animals.
By Christer Eriksson, Susan Lumpkin, and John Seidensticker. Time Life Books, 1995.

Living Monsters: The World's Most Dangerous Animals.
By Howard Tomb. Simon & Schuster, 1990.

The Usborne World of Animals.
By Susanna Davidson and Mike Unwin. Usborne Books, 2005.

The Way Nature Works.
Edited by Jill Bailey. MacMillan Publishing Company, 1997.

For Robin — S.J.

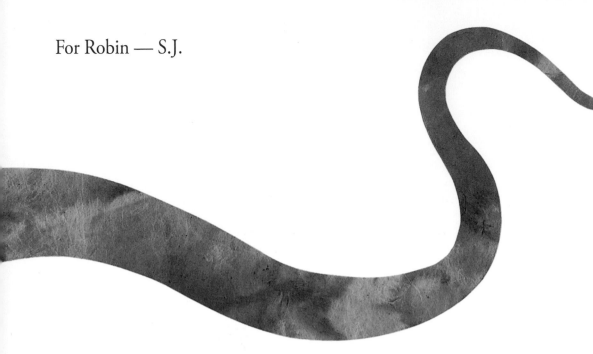

All rights reserved. Originally published in hardcover in the United States by Houghton Mifflin Books for Children, an imprint of Houghton Mifflin Harcourt Publishing Company, 2009.

For information about permission to reproduce selections from this book, write to trade.permissions@hmhco.com or to Permissions, Houghton Mifflin Harcourt Publishing Company, 3 Park Avenue, 19th Floor, New York, New York 10016.

www.hmhco.com

The text of this book is set in Adobe Garamond Pro.
The illustrations are collages of cut and torn paper.

Library of Congress Cataloging-in-Publication data is on file.

ISBN: 978-0-618-96620-2 hardcover
ISBN: 978-0-544-22801-6 paperback

Manufactured in China
SCP 25 24 23 22 21 20 19 18 17

4500821780